EMPTY
CLIP

AKRON SERIES IN POETRY

AKRON SERIES IN POETRY

Mary Biddinger, Editor

Emilia Phillips, *Empty Clip*
Anne Barngrover, *Brazen Creature*
Matthew Guenette, *Vasectomania*
Sandra Simonds, *Further Problems with Pleasure*
Leslie Harrison, *The Book of Endings*
Emilia Phillips, *Groundspeed*
Philip Metres, *Pictures at an Exhibition: A Petersburg Album*
Jennifer Moore, *The Veronica Maneuver*
Brittany Cavallaro, *Girl-King*
Oliver de la Paz, *Post Subject: A Fable*
John Repp, *Fat Jersey Blues*
Emilia Phillips, *Signaletics*
Seth Abramson, *Thievery*
Steve Kistulentz, *Little Black Daydream*
Jason Bredle, *Carnival*
Emily Rosko, *Prop Rockery*
Alison Pelegrin, *Hurricane Party*
Matthew Guenette, *American Busboy*
Joshua Harmon, *Le Spleen de Poughkeepsie*

Titles published since 2010.
For a complete listing of titles published in the series,
go to www.uakron.edu/uapress/poetry.

EMPTY CLIP

EMILIA PHILLIPS

 The University of Akron Press
Akron, Ohio

ISBN: 978-1-629220-99-4 (paper)
ISBN: 978-1-629221-00-7 (ePDF)
ISBN: 978-1-629221-01-4 (ePub)

Library of Congress Cataloging-in-Publication Data
  Names: Phillips, Emilia, author.
Title: Empty clip / Emilia Phillips.
Description: First edition. | Akron, Ohio : The University of Akron Press, 2018. | Series:
  Akron series in poetry |
Identifiers: LCCN 2017051217 (print) | LCCN 2017054840 (ebook) | ISBN
  9781629221007 (ePDF) | ISBN 9781629221014 (ePub) | ISBN 9781629220994
  (paper : alk. paper)
Classification: LCC PS3616.H4553 (ebook) | LCC PS3616.H4553 A6 2018 (print) |
  DDC 811/.6–dc23
LC record available at https://lccn.loc.gov/2017051217

∞The paper used in this publication meets the minimum requirements of ANSI/NISO
z39.48–1992 (Permanence of Paper).

Cover image: *Can't Forget, Won't Forget* by Rhed Fawell. Cover design by Amy Freels.

Empty Clip was designed and typeset in New Baskerville by Amy Freels and printed on
sixty-pound natural and bound by Bookmasters of Ashland, Ohio.

CONTENTS

FOR JOEY KINGSLEY AND LENA MOSES-SCHMITT

Let heaven and men and devils, let them all,
All, all, cry shame against me, yet I'll speak.

—EMILIA IN *OTHELLO*

THIS IS HOW I CAME TO KNOW HOW TO

forget afternoons   crying after St.

Kindergarten, not what happens but who
makes them

        happen. The Red-

Haired Man. *Lie down*,
said the grass to the sky. *Lie down*, said time

to the roof. A memory of a memory, and then

the memory

     I didn't

remember until I was asked *if, to*—   I'm playing

with a cutaway
      dollhouse, the others

asleep on their blue   pallets, the corners

of the sweet boy's mouth

crumbed, his eyelashes candid as what we hide
from ourselves. My arm loosens,
               my weight,

      my weight   falling from my earthward

hips, legs unfolding, to my feet as I'm lifted, he lifts

me up, the doll dropping

top-heavy from my hand, her hair   frayed, my soles'

     duplicitous shadow in the dim

window light gauzed
by sheer

curtains that rise—   *Lie down,* said the ear to

the whisper. *Lie down,* said

the dark to the anchorite

     light the door   opened upon

     as he swung
     me into the kitchen

     whose song is coffee burbling and gossip

except there's no
one now

this afternoon, the pantry full   of graham crackers and Peter
     Pan

peanut butter, the bare

     bulb is

on. Then it is   off. *Lie*

down, the teacher said
to the children. *Lie down,* the life

     to the lie—
     the school denies

a man like that
ever working there. Lie down in the length

of your body, which is more
linear than
time. He bolted   the door. No,

you may not come   in, no

you may
not   come in, knuckles

on the door frame, freckles decimaled beneath his backhand's

coppery hairs. Lie   down.
Lie. Lay down the life

to the lie. Where?
Will you? Pleat

of khakis,
          braid

of belt. No, I will not. You may not

come in. This is how I came to
          know how

to forget.
          Lie down, said the whisper
to the ear,
                    said the grass
to the sky.
          The teacher

to the students: *Now rest
          your eyes.*

HOLLOW POINT

TO THE NEIGHBOR BOY WITH HIS FATHER'S HUNTING RIFLE, BEGGING THE POLICE TO SHOOT

Your name is an empty clip
the local news wants to load

with rumors of substance
abuse. *Disturbed*, next

door says over the fence as he pushes
his mower into the shed

after the borough's door-
to-door order to stay

in. The streets went dark first
with SWAT, their helmets sun-

glossed to mirror. They looked
bored this far down, kicking dirt

& wiping palm sweat
on the Kevlar over

their hearts. Later, something else
rolled in—not dark

exactly. It was still
afternoon, & I walked

out on my porch but wasn't
turned back. I heard you, faint

& guttered to nonsense
by the hot wind,

but I couldn't see you. Blocked
by vans, I watched instead

the tree in your parents' yard
sway, turning out its leaves

like wrists, the air a-hiss
with radios, & still

no black clouds.
No dark rain.

HOLLOW POINT

I found my shoe print
in blood once—
after I walked in
on the murder
scene of my dog,
my stepfather in the bathroom
cleaning his gun.

I knew something of mercy then
and how it can be unjust,

the way the dog's head opened
like laughter
into grief, the hollow points
screaming skull and brain
into the dining room wall.

Afterwards, he gathered the dog's shadow
in black garbage bag
and stuffed into the trunk to heave
into the church
dumpster. For a moment, I
was only animal,

not because of any excess
projected point blank into me,
but because I'm almost always
animal anyway. See, I nearly broke

the nurse's hand years later
when she held me down
for the radiologist to inject
radioactive contrast eight times along
my cheekbone and jaw, its heat
angry as brakes on a train—

hurt her because I was being hurt,
hurt her because
hurting was a way for me
to forget or forgive
my angry love.

BEFORE HOTEL SECURITY GOT THERE

From the half-lidded reverie of whiskey I'd masked

as *sleep*, the sound of body on body on headboard

on a wall came to me first as *fucking*, illicit, her moan

pleasure—so then I might have touched myself,

as I sometimes do when I can't quite wake and I can't quite

sleep, before I remembered my friend in the second

queen. But who doesn't love the unrequitedness

of the self, its question answered with a question? Our Newark

non-smoking room rising then out of timelessness

into time as the TV's blue wraith hop-skip-jumped

brainwaves into a circadian dawn as a lamp/vase/champagne

flute burst into a kind of song and the lovers became

sudden hulks brawling, rendered concrete by the weight

they threw against the wall.

OVERPASS

Not high enough for suicide
                or low for easy landing, save for
                        the cinematic timing of a feline

                leap onto the back of a passing
                        semi. Not that I've considered it—
                        but my eyes have,

                and in this way I've sent my energies into
                        the possibilities,

                                        like dogs after
                                        the Missing

                into the ravine of time. As a child, I watched
                                the funnel
                        cake-fat catfish disappear under the park's

        footbridge

and reappear on the other side, as the twin
        barracudas of headlights current
                                now into the black
                                expressway like nostalgia. I'm ready to say
                                        that whatever
        holds

                        our attention is a brief
                god, that Americans have many, that lovers can be glorified;
                                that stopping with my hands
                                in my ratty pea coat pockets

                        here is reverence for my own life, even if
I measure it against its impact

                              on the pavement. I don't know
              any songs the wind also doesn't. I'd sing them—
                                        but I better get back

                                        home. I walk buckled
brick into the neighborhood, Sunday

quiet. Framed in the windows
above the back doors are green bottles
collecting dust. Sometimes I glimpse
a silhouette & know
                        someone's home. The more we speak of the
   world,
the more it becomes concrete

& metaphor. So let me stop here—

at the back gate of the dark yard that surrounds the house filled
with light and the music of a body's weight going
                                up the stairs. I could almost
   believe the world
                        would give me another

   life by the way a streetlight files
                        the house's shadow
                                to darken down my boots.

CAMPUS SHOOTER POWERPOINT AND INFORMATION SESSION

The font, Chiller—
blood dripping, its un-bodily
red meant to impress spectacular
consequence. Modeling
projection (*I on you*) through
projection (*light
on surface*). The point-blank image
focused on the barrel blurred
cameo-like at the edges. They
mean, they say, to give us a plan—
a route, procedure, a way
out but the *phck, phck, phck*
of the Fx as bullet holes animate
over the text causes the prof
next to me to flinch, startled
away from his Words
with Friends board. A siren
tsunamis now out of the PA—
its crackle and hiss legionous
as it drowns out the security
chief's voice who keeps on
talking so I must strain
to hear his litany
of stats. A retired cop
like my father, who has the same
stiff casualness of someone
pretending they're not on guard
while they say they are always
on guard. I think of my father's
lapses in small talk when we
entered my grandmother's favorite
restaurant while he scanned
the room pretending to look

for a waiter or bathroom as he
swept every face at every table for
anyone he ever arrested or
testified against. Videos now, first hands
from Umpqua and Virginia
Tech and So On. And this
subliminal with tense shifts,
the scroll of campuses in red
on black moving so fast it's
illegible, but I try to read at least
one, the So On accurate
in its imprecision, its inability
to witness in full. *If a shooter
enters your classroom, there's nothing
I can do*, he says, loosening his
tie. *But I can help the classroom next
door.* An aerial of our
campus, a handgun moving
in a translucent corona
of red from one building
where I teach to another
where my office is. My
father sat outside
my first job in his unmarked
car whenever I closed
and would only leave
when he saw me locking up.
He never told me. Never
waved. Sat in shadow. How I
thought the So On then
might be an urging of instinct, of will,
an *I'll keep you safe even if you
wrench away*, but now,
when the chief says, *We really don't
know what could happen and so
we don't have a set
script*, the So On
seems to take
shape after

shape after shape,
the way we are always
moving into all the bodies
we have and are
in our lives. The So On
in the day-to-day's scope
playing dead,
but its pulse quick,
animal, alive.

TO THE PREVIOUS TENANT

On the overhead
        beams in the basement

I found the hypodermics

        stolen from your diabetic
mother—or that's the story

        I've offered—

and, behind the loose brick
on the wall behind the well, the pipe
        rigged

from an Advil bottle

        punctured and fitted
with a ballpoint pen's halved

        shell, a crude carb hatched
in, the top limned
in aluminum foil. The papers
        stuffed on the spare bedroom

closet's shelf tell of lost
        custody and back child
support. Unemployment, and delinquent court

        appearances. I've kept

a pile of your summons
        and collection notes
in a box by the front door,

as if you might return
for something you left—

a hidden stash, a home, an idea

of self. But I should warn you

the police have stopped by
twice now, and I told them
I don't know
you, but I'm not so sure

anymore. Sometimes
when I'm pushing
my cart through the Giant

past the gentle
mist on parsley and the thunder
sound

on a crackly speaker, I wonder
if I'd recognize you

if we met in the bread aisle
or at the automatic sliding door.
I've given you

a hair color
and style, a ball cap frayed
at the bill, but I don't know

your eyes—
you squint so much
in my imagination of you.
But I do too, at the mirror—

the right cheek slack and hatched
in scar. The detective said you renewed

your driver's license
            with my address. So I take the dog out
to the old chicken coop to sniff,
                and think, if he takes to a smell,
        we've got you.

But he just hikes

and whizzes, the snow steaming

where it hits. I leave
        a light on

for you most nights, but I don't know if I would
        meet you

with warning
        shots from the inherited pistol,
or a bowl of leftovers. Some nights,
you're as distant as

before, but others, as I do

        the dishes alone—
I find a space
        for you

at the tree line, in the long-gone

        where you're hiding. There

you are, I say. There
        you are, right there. As close
as you'll ever get, as far
away.

DENOUEMENT

That winter I was afraid of death
and so wished it upon myself.

The water sluggishly boiled
against the salt, but when it roiled

I didn't want
to eat and turned it off.

The snow was up to my knees.
The shovel handle cracked in two.

The nuclear plant high-rised
steam. It was the most heavenlike thing

I've ever seen. One doesn't have to
believe in symbols

to see them. I waited on results,
to piss out the last of the opiates.

When the dog sniffed,
I wondered if it was a pronouncement—

she liked to roll on rotten things
after all. I watched

TV until I couldn't
sleep. I watched

the snow on the other side
of the screen door.

I didn't eat for days.
I worried until it was a kind of prayer.

I watched the dark,
my eyes focus and unfocus

in the mirror. Through this
I thought I might live forever.

APOSTROPHE, OREGON HILL

Out to the curb with the couch
    that in rain-swell will sweeten to musk
        and mildew. How do you make a life again

out of an empty room? Out the faceless
    spectres dance from the brake-hiss
        bus into the back alleys where flies rearrange

on a compost of corn husks and orange
    rinds, where a sentence is as long as the power lines
        framed by a window. The chains clatter

with the hoarse dogs' charges toward
    the foot-sound of gravel, the rattle
        of cicadas and Harleys cruising Idlewood,

as the trains owl along the James, warped
    by distance and movement, the sedate heartbeat
        of a record spent in exhaustible meditation on what's

the same, what's changed, how our lives bend
    like light through the atmosphere and arrive
        blue and hazy. I always thought the night was yours,

and gave it to you in indulgences: the zigzag home
    of a fluid black dress and leather boots, your
        hair under a streetlamp the color of a rolly's

cherry on the updraft. A laugh around
    the corner, a siren—and then one came urging
        you into the sterile lean-to of the Found-Lurkings,

its fluorescent revelations tempered
    by the four-headed friend in the waiting
        room who crushed creamers into worry's unending

black coffee. I'll never know the night
        that sat upon you like the hag or the hook
                of thought that set in your ear like a murder

ballad, but while you were gone, I stayed among
        your things, and unraveled the evenings
                into burnt percolators and the cut deck of words

and long walks with your wolf-dog
        on which I was heckled by the holdouts' slur-song
                of sagging porches, where I gave over, where I gave in

to your absence dense inside me as fulgurite
        in sand after a lightning
                storm. I turned toward the thought

of you as a crowd in shadow toward a soloist
        when the solo begins. Don't think the voice isn't
                lonely when it sings. I tried to bring you back

in some echo's hollowing, but my voice was thin,
        the air humid, and the silhouettes at the bus stops slumped
                as a to-go box oozed beside the empty red high-tops

on the stoop of Carter's boarded-up Novelty Store.
        Where was I to go where you weren't?
        Where was I to go where you were?

and now that you've returned to
        discard things destroyed in the far-
                afield, your room has room for light,

that in the morning I hope will cast your shadow
        away from you rather than bury it
                like a sword in your side.

ON A LATE-NIGHT ENCOUNTER WITH A BAREFOOT COLLEGE STUDENT WEARING ONLY A PARTY DRESS AND A MAN'S BLAZER

For blocks my shadow held her
and when I turned, she jumped

behind a telephone pole or a wall
until she decided she wanted me to know,

feet slapping the pavement as she came up

behind me and put her hands
over my eyes to say "guess who"

I greeted her as if nothing was
wrong, but asked what she was doing

and where she'd come from

Her words, beveled edges,
her sentences uroboric—

A party   A jerk   Day drinking

then all of a sudden it was
night and she wanted to

walk alone, like a haunt

I offered to drive her home
My friends, to buy her something to eat

"Can we go to your house
and hang out?" she asked   "I don't want to

go back"

No   No, but let's get you home
No, but I think you're done

She wanted to keep walking then
if I was going to be like that

The town locked up, windows
light-quiet

except for the Lincoln Diner, 7-11, and the frats

spilled onto the lawns and Battlefield
park and campus   twos and threes passing

with jeers when her dress fell down
and revealed her

We pulled it back up   I thought of her classmate's

poem about a girl
getting raped by a soccer player then

We insisted We got saltines and Advil and ginger ale
at the 7-11 and we got her in the car

The poem was about a freshman who had gone
to a party and has had a hard time

leaving since,
another girl in the class said, "Girls

get raped all the time here   I don't know why
this time was so special"

After class I cried in my office

We offered to take my student

to the campus police or home—

her choice   She cried in the back seat wanting

to know if I was going to fail her
I said I wasn't   I didn't

but in truth I really don't know

NOCTURNE, LAMAR'S CHRYSTAL LOUNGE

Up the astroturfed
steps our sight to stars condenses
    to a vinyl
portico, green, aglow
      with cursive

Park in Rear—
    an offensive to the solid
order of a city
      in the dark, but once
inside we grope

    through the restaurant,
booth-humped
      in shadow, and down
the hall to a small
    lounge, crushed

velvet on the walls
      in blackberry-colored
chandeliers embossed
    on bronze, as oil
lamps flicker between

    the two-seaters
like pheromones. Sometimes
    I can do anything
with an excuse. Half
      permission, half

pardoning. The night
    I lost, one I'll never
lose. I can't deepen
        the darkness
behind my eyes, slow-

    dancing alone
to Dinah, or hide
        in one of the busted-
up bathroom stalls. Here
    I'm made of words

even if once I was made
        of matter and am
now, somewhere
    else. Do you hear
that song? That vibrato—

    a gin-burn
laughed into the nose.
    I grind
a thumbnail on the side
        of a quarter

in my pocket as I lean into
    Gerald's offered
light.

ONE YEAR AFTER
CONTEMPLATING SUICIDE

—after Erika L. Sánchez

Admit it—
the end returns to you

yet, like a stitch
meant to dissolve

that works its way
out, that blistery

worm—

Once you think
you're healed,

what heals turns
against you—

a tourniquet left on too long.

But you know how close
you could still come,

don't you? Last night you saw
it in the mirror

where you held your head

to your shadow
and saw

your eyes seeing your eyes

seeing. Sometimes it comes like desire,
the way the smell

of some soap turns you
back into a body—

the body that wanted that body
that needed only

an idea of you. Sometimes the light

scours away the future
into which you survive still,

a dirt road
mile-markered by loss, loss

in your idea of the scar

your cheek shrugs. How ideas fit
you, weight

and itch, like a slip

of shame under your skirt.
Yes, it was

a gun—
because it's how your father

taught you all things end.

Although you imagined
its pull easy as that from the wet mother

gin,

you saw something
didn't you? It burst
from you blood blister
bought and paid for by
the heedless flesh
selfish to keep its

demise locked compacted
slowed by the very matter
of you close
like an enemy close
like a child inside but its trajectory

greys the divide

between you and those you love
those few who love you

barreling into them
maybe not bullet but its babel
breaking open like the sun
of some notion to its internal
bleed yellow

SPLIT SCREEN

"THE DAYS THAT WERE HAVE NOW"

—Gilgamesh

in all eyes a witness.
In every mouth, lies. The truth is
a broken bone that can't be
set. Tender are the breasts' proprietary
bruises from the steering
wheel. Nothing is more sexual
than being trapped. Just ask,

and a politician will sign anything,
even a cast. The body's made
real through habit, the body's made
real through habit. Two blips
meet on the street, in love or conspiracy—
motives so close from 60
thousand feet, they're almost

indistinguishable. Dear G-O
-D, dear satellites; dear
Voyager and able dead
light: no lyric exists anymore
except in the spam folder. Perhaps our secrets are
safest with those we don't know. In all
eyes a witness. In every lie,

a mouth. After the accident
one man will say to another,
She could be bleeding internally,
don't move her.

THE CIA LIVE-TWEETS THE ASSASSINATION OF USAMA BIN LADIN FIVE YEARS LATER

> *To mark the 5th anniversary of the Usama Bin Ladin operation in Abbottabad we will tweet the raid as if it were happening today. #UBLRaid*
> *—@CIA, May 1, 2016, 1:22 p.m.*

because repetition

makes muscle

makes muscle
memory

of violence

the dead make us

alive or so

we tell them

we tell them
to tell us

would we know

otherwise would we

know how to
know if not

for what we leave
unknown

unknown
because *re* means

again   regarding
reply   because

how can we remember
to hold our tongues

when we've lost
our heads say the dead

we have them

because 2.3k have given their hearts
I go to report them

& I'm asked *How is @CIA being abusive or harmful?*
Who is @CIA targeting?
    —*Me*
    —*Someone else*

because I need an all of the above
because what they want us distracted from
becomes the distraction

casualties become casual
become causality

in autocorrect

to say that the dead know
their place is to say we

have put them there

have put them there

have put them there

have put them there

have put them there

THE UNCANNY VALLEY

*"The body of the user in a virtual environment is a complex
structure, a subject-object . . . it is a quasi-cyborg body . . . a body
that translates itself into an eminently active spectral entity."*
—Roberto Diodato, The Aesthetics of the Virtual

"Yea, though I walk through the valley in the shadow of death . . ."

How moon the new
      moon
          over the uncanny
   valley, that vixening

vertigo of simulacra
      simpatico
         with the mind's
  conflation & eye's

aphasia of detail
      & human
          complication. Here
  I stand on the street

corner, doubled—
      self
         shoulder-winged
  like all the fallen

egos newly made
      mortal, &, again,
         in reductive code, a blue
  dot nosed by an arrow

where I'm facing,
      the surrounding
         buildings rendered
  by shadow & shade, verging

3D, their ghost
        perspective
                overlaying the bleed
    of neither-here

nor-there. Where
        falls
                my shadow from
    my avatar? Where

lies my ear except
        doppelgänged
                on either side
    of my melon, that

volted variable?
        The doppler
                effect of the past
    leaves memory

as flat as a brass
        note
                from a horn expanded
    in the heat. The mirror

silvers a circuitry
        of *me,*
                that's me, I
    think. What's almost

human damns us by its
        error
                of no error, even this palpable
    me in my palm. I belong

to the darkness of
        the world—
                its haloing street-
    lights, the dog

barking to tell me
          there
                are still
     distances I can cross

with my feet, my
          hope
                like a blister
     on my heel, as I try

to find my way
          back
                to the hotel. How
     blood the blood

of the metaphor,
          how still
                the heart that's
     beaten in fear.

PICA OF UNSAID THINGS

Yes, I swallowed them.
Those bitter bolts rust in acidic
afterthought. This tetanus
of tautology turns my gut a copper
gangrene, a belfry
swallowed. Did you know passive
aggression is so soluble?
A soapy mouth learns other ways
to speak: homonymic hymns
of *lye* & *lie*. The awful offal
becomes my loden, stinking.
Anger uncomplicates. But I gulped
the wrong way. I am a glutton
for bile. I make drinking
songs of silence. Chugalug catgut.
& choke it back. Wolf
down this *I can't, I won't*—
this *yes, yes, I mean, don't.*

BARISTA

—*after Laura Kasischke*

Andrew, an evening regular, rattled

the mint tin he presented from his pocket like a carat
promise or faith in the face

of doubt, and set it on the counter
where I counted tills, replacing payday
twenties for coin rolls and lower

denominations. "I did this
for you," he said, Herod Antipas to my oblivious

Salome. He asks me to
open the box, and so I do—to chalk-

white burrs, four, from pencil
eraser to the size of a sugar

cube. Kidney stones.

Of course, my co-workers' voices slur

on the head-
set: "Oh, Emilia, I want
to show you where these

passed." But I'm only a server then, a junior

in college who's learned less about
saying *no* than how to seduce
bills into the tip jar from men's

wallets that smell animal, like a horse

that sweat under the heat
of a saddle that once rocked me flushed and wet before I'd ever been

fucked—
All these ways our phrases twin toward
opposites. He looked

expectant, his eyes always
reflective as if he were crying but not

letting go
of the salt,

the way one fragments, reassigns
part of one's own body to

become the body
of the lover one desires
but cannot have
in a room alone tonight, window open, not so much

with a distance between them, but

within that distance,
which is amnesiac as horizon and blue
in the way we say water

is blue, although it has
no color except in its depths. I wanted

to say *yes*
then, if only so that our humiliation
was complicit, a coat
in which we each had an arm. My boss

leaned his shoulder
into mine and whispered, "Is this guy
bothering you?"
but the sun was
setting, and the milk hissing under the steam wands like a white

mouse with fangs set
in it, and there is no other devotion
as real as separateness. I
tossed off a joke about how unhealthy I was
for him, which he liked. Just months

before I'd pleaded with
a tweaked-out vagrant to stop
snorting the Splendas
and Equals he
ripped and poured
out on the condiment
bar. But when I asked

him to leave, he said he
couldn't because
I couldn't see him—he was

invisible, or not there at

all, he insisted, as he started for
the Sweet-n-Lows. I didn't

see Andrew for a long time after
he brought his gift, and after closing,

I quietly stacked the safe full
of what we'd earned
and then chained together the chairs
on the patio, picking

up cigarettes butts with my bare
fingers so I could smell the razored acridity later as I fell
asleep without feeling

guilty. But the wind, strong

from the west in
warning, like all ineffable forces,
gave me back

my body—my belly sour, all rewind
and glower, the way
memory of grief has no cause, only the lyric
shove that sends the ground

up to us, fuming the
smell of rain, ozone, grain—
He spit on the sidewalk

as he left. When I
told him to put his ruins away and turned to get his usual, I

thought I heard him say, "Emilia, you *will*

love me," and, playing toward my pocket money, I said, "Is that

a promise?" I said: "I already do."

FINGERS IN A THROAT

Because
lack feeds
on lack
the body turns
out
what is not
yet body
or shit.
You

were
excused
from chorus to wet
your mouth
at the water
fountain, but not
just for
song
but heave, your

belly
has grown
taut. When
someone else
comes in
the girls'
room, you

hold
the retched-up
in your mouth
until it sours
your nose.

You've learned
        to keep
saline
        spray

        and spearmint
toothpaste
        and the cheap
Curve
        perfume
in your
            purse.

        You know every
girl by her
        ankle,
that crescent
        shadow
under bone, their
        shoe-
                laces,

        the way
their weight
        molds the uniform
shoe. You know
        how long
and if they pause
        at the mirror, more
slender
        in how

        they are
rendered
        by the frosted
glass, each dark
        anonymous,
lashed across
        the floor
to the stall
                door.

FACESOFDEATH.COM

On my grandmother's PC monitor
    the size of a Butterball

turkey with its dial-up modem like Casio

    keyboard trumpets cut with a razor

on glass, my cousin, a half
    year older

    than me, pulled up the website, slow

to boot—first the black
    background and the gallery

outline of thumbnails

    and red links to categorize Causes: Car

Crashes, Gunshot, Suicide, some
    duplicated across tallies. The logo,

last to arrive: a pixelated

    shock font. Blood dripping or as if slashed

into skin—I can't
    remember. We kept something

else open in case someone

    else walked in, cartoons on in the living

room and our parents with second
    or third helpings. I saw the faces,

hollow eyes wide, and I looked

for blood, and I looked away

from blood, and I looked at my cousin
to realize then that he would die

and that anyone could—

First cousin, first friend,

first person I lost touch with, now
just a photo in my Facebook

newsfeed: camo and a rifle,

a shotgun, a .44 with a

silencer.
Buckshot, BB, some high caliber

slug. The voicemail

from my stepmother: *Your father's*

been shot. Not *how.* Not *alive*
or *dead.* I called again and again

until someone, anyone

picked up. An accident—he did it

to himself, and the tourniquet.
His tongue slugged by morphine, he said

on the phone, *I don't want this*

to deter you from owning

a gun. He said, *I'll buy you*
    one. I said no. I said, *No.* I said,

I have my grandfather's service

    sidearm just to button up

the issue. I admit I wondered
    what it would be like to hold

the barrel between my teeth

    back when I was looking down the barrel

of days of grief,
    but *statistically women don't shoot*

themselves. I remember one

victim—was it suicide or murder?

    Does it matter?—how the bullet

grooved clean into the skin below
    her clavicle. A buttonhole, a baby's

mouth. No. A window, a rose,

    the space into which someone goes.

SCAR

Sometimes it's
      bigger than my
       body, the body

that gave it
      life, that *is*
       its life—as if I'm

a frame for
      it, as if it
       continues beyond

my end, although no
      one, not here,
       can see where

it goes, how
      far, and now
       it finds

its way into
      every possible
       place I

imagine, even
      the past, which believes
       in my scar like

a prophecy, and like a god's
      work, I have no
       memory of it breathing

into me and
      abstracting me
       to myth from which to

remake the world
.......into the rising
.........and falling

action of fiction—my body
.........as denouement. Sometimes I feel
...........it without waiting

for its hum on
.........the nerves, its shivering
...........arc from eye

to jawbone. How often
.........I want to
...........give it a voice so

it can tell
.........me what I want
...........it to say—that it knows

me like tomorrow
.........does. That a need lives
...........in lack's *because.*

ON RECEIPT OF A DICK PIC

We wanted arrival to be instant
because we didn't want to be separate
from what we loved.
—Dana Levin

My imagination is generous, but my resolution is not
I wanted to say. Become an unknown number, a crank
call before this fragment diminished in the cis-binary
of phallic ones, vaginal zeros. All bodies are anachronisms,
always dragging the club feet of their conceptions into future
after future after future immured in *now*. I wish we could say
we are making ourselves eternal by making ourselves
forwardable, an afterlife in the cloud. How like the *Assunta*
the Singularity, which always seemed like some Oedipal paraphilia.
But you have made your tongue into the letter *p*, your eyes
into a colon. I have always wanted to name a cock
"Pun," a word derived from the Italians' raunchy-noised
punctilio (its fuck-sound in the compound consonant
entering a slippery *el*), but all it means: a fine or petty point
of conduct or procedure. We will never forgive one another
for being human, which is a part of what makes us
human. I opened the image in the sun so bright
I had to shade the screen from what reductions of me
instinct makes. My nude, my spam, my beloved, Titian was
called "The Sun Amidst Small Stars." But how does one love
what's made of light and so far away?

SELF-PORTRAIT WITHOUT A BODY

Volatile vesper flamed
                    to fallow

            the space between

      one *I* slash

                  you and another. Come hither,

            nether. Sexual dark

      matter: neither *nor*

nor *or*, either idea—

      or elemental

      et al. Object

      lesson in

abstraction, seen

      best when un-

                  seen. A question

                  answered with
                              a question—

            a phantom

      ache, instinctual

stint. Can never

leave

      because was

no, is   *never.* The periphery:

  capable

incapability, a future

    perfect verb.
       Nerve now

verve that urges
    the verge. *Else* or *erst-*

        while. A breath

    without lung. Open air. Still.

DREAM OF THE PHONE BOOTH

My story's told in the mis-dial's
hesitance and anonyms of crank calls,

in the wires' electric elegy
and glass expanded by the moth

flicker of filament. I call a past
that believes I'm dead. On the concrete

here, you can see where
I stood in rust, lashed to the grid.

On the corner of Pine and Idlewood,
I've seen a virgin on her knees

before the angel
of a streetlight and Moses stealing the *Times*

to build a fire. I've seen the city fly
right through a memory and not break

its neck. But the street still needs a shrine,
so return my ringing heart and no one

to answer it, a traveler whose only destination is
waywardness. Forgive us

our apologies, the bees in our bells, the receiver's
grease, days horizoned

into words. If we stand
monument to anything,

it's that only some voices belong
to men.

Notes

The book's epigraph is spoken by Emilia in Act V of *Othello*. She has realized Iago's treachery, and she defies the male characters' warnings not to speak out against her husband.

p. 9
"Hollow Point" is named after a type of bullet.

p. 25
"On a Late-Night Encounter with a Barefoot College Student Wearing Only a Party Dress and a Man's Blazer" was written with many thanks to R.T. and J.E.

p. 28
If you're ever in Chattanooga, Tennessee, go to Lamar's at 1018 E. MLK Blvd.

p. 30
"One Year After Contemplating Suicide" is after Erika L. Sánchez's "Six Months After Contemplating Suicide."

p. 40
"Barista" is after Laura Kasischke's "Hostess."

p. 51
"On Receipt of a Dick Pic" takes its epigraph from Dana Levin's "Across the Sea."

ACKNOWLEDGMENTS

This book was written in order to live. Thank you to all those—friends, family, mentors, poets, and otherwise—who helped me do so. I'm also grateful to those at the University of Akron Press who helped this book have its own life.

Thank you to the journals that previously published these poems, sometimes in earlier versions:

BOAAT Journal: "This is how I came to know how to"
Boston Review: "'The days that were have now'"
Cherry Tree: "Apostrophe, Oregon Hill"
The Collapsar: "facesofdeath.com," "Fingers in a Throat," and "To the Previous Tenant"
Foundry: "Pica of Unsaid Things" and "Self-Portrait Without a Body"
Horsethief: "The CIA Live-tweets the Assassination of Usama Bin Ladin Five Years Later"
Lunch: "To the Neighbor Boy with His Father's Hunting Rifle, Begging the Police to Shoot"
Memorious: "Nocturne, Lamar's Chrystal Lounge" and "Overpass"
Muzzle: "On Receipt of a Dick Pic"
Poem-a-Day from the Academy of American Poets: "Scar"
Poetry: "Dream of the Phone Booth"
South Dakota Review: "Hollow Point," "Campus Shooter Powerpoint and Information Session," and "Before Hotel Security Got There"

Photo: Tracy Tanner

Emilia Phillips is the author of two other poetry collec-
tions from the University of Akron Press, *Signaletics*
(2013) and *Groundspeed* (2016), and three chapbooks.
Her poems and lyric essays appear widely in literary
publications including *Agni, Boston Review, Ploughshares,
Poetry*, and elsewhere. She's an assistant professor in the
MFA Writing Program and the Department of English
at the University of North Carolina at Greensboro.